How to
Not Quit Your Ministry

by Michael Cavanaugh

ISBN 978-1-945423-20-8

For worldwide distribution
Printed in the USA

Table of Contents

A Sad Headline

The headline in the local paper read,

"Minister Thought Dead Discovered in California."

This came from an actual newspaper, and it is an interesting story. We don't know exactly what happened on that particular day, but at the end of a workday, a pastor took his car and drove it down to a river. They found that he had taken his shoes off and placed them by the edge of the river, so people naturally assumed that he had committed suicide. His family had a funeral at the church, and everybody's heart was broken for the whole situation. But what was really shocking came two years later, when one of the parishioners was getting on a bus — and the pastor who was thought dead was there alive.

My experience is that, over the course of a person's time in ministry, there are lots of different pressures we face that can cause us to come to the place — not necessarily to do what this man did, but in a similar way — where we drive to the river and take our shoes off. There are some pastors I know whose only reason they are still in the pulpit is economic pressure. The fact is they are no longer present in their hearts; even though they still show up to church every Sunday, their shoes have been left by the river.

I want to talk with you about that crisis moment in your ministry life.

9 Reasons People Might Quit the Ministry

There are several different pressure points that can contribute to our trip to the edge of the river.

1. *PERSONAL EVALUATION OF YOUR CALLING AND EFFECTIVENESS*

Let me explain. Many of us have watched American Idol, the television singing competition. My favorite part of American Idol is not the end where the winner is crowned, though that can be very dramatic and exciting, but my really favorite part is the first three or four shows when they have all the people who sincerely believe they can sing but are terrible. You know what I'm talking about; you're sitting there and you hear the person sing and they are absolutely terrible. Then the judges say to them, "I'm sorry, Honey. It's just not going to work this time." And then you watch the person walk out of the room, face filled with frustration and muttering under their breath, "I know I have it. I know I'll be a star." And you're thinking, "This person needs a reality check."

Have you ever thought that maybe you were that person when it came to the ministry? That if we had American Idol for Ministry, you would be the guy/gal to whom the four judges would be saying, "No. No, you are not going on," and you'd be storming out of the room muttering, "I know I'm the one who is going to win it." But when you look at it on television, you are thinking to yourself, "How could anybody be so self-deceived about their ability to sing? Don't they have any friends?" I saw one show where the contestant's mother was with her child who couldn't sing. I wanted to take the mother aside and say, "Tell your child the truth!" Instead, the mother was putting her arm around her daughter and comforting her by saying, "I don't understand these judges. You're great. You can do it. I love to hear you sing at home."

In ministry we can come to these moments of self-doubt, where we look at ourselves and we start to wonder... Am I that one? Am I that guy? I thought I was called to ministry, but am I really? Am I that woman who thought she had a ministry, but as I come to face my struggles with effectiveness, I'm questioning my call? Maybe I just don't have any friends with the courage to step up and tell me, "Give it up, stop it right now, because it is not working."

One pastor said it this way, "It's hard to feel significant as a pastor. We are constantly compared to amazing speakers, incredible entrepreneurs and holy, monkish people who pray more than we can. Our churches are compared to huge churches with massive budgets, and incredible bands, and staffs as large as our whole congregation."

One of the great questions we face when we are processing our confidence in our call to ministry is our desire for significance. This is especially the case if the field of ministry that the Lord has given us seems small. I think one of the things we don't understand many times about God is how extravagant He is. We think that because God sends us to a little community that we must be a puny person. "If God chose me to go to this small town, it must be because I have few gifts, little ability and negligible capacity, and the reason I've been given this tiny mission is because I don't have the potential for anything else."

I see this as total misunderstanding of God. If I were the one guiding your life, that might be the right evaluation, because I would always have to be guided by efficiency. I'm a limited person; therefore, I would need to put limited people in limited situations to be efficient. I would always decide things based on what gave the most efficient result.

But God is not efficient. God is all powerful, and therefore God can be extravagant! God will take a premium person, a person filled with spiritual gifts, filled with all kinds of capacity, and He'll take that person and say, "I am going to sow you into these 50 people. I'm going to pour your life into them. Because I love them so much, I'm willing to send you to them."

I remember early in my ministry when the Lord was challenging me about going to a small community to serve the people there. As I was arguing with Him over His obvious lack of appreciation for my gifts and abilities, the Lord just spoke to me and said, "If you will allow me to bury you, I will do more with your life in 5 years than you could do with 50 years of your own effort." Sometimes we don't realize that God has buried us in a place and that He has purposes and objectives that are not immediately visible and are far beyond our comprehension.

I think sometimes when we go through a time of personal evaluation of our call and effectiveness, in our hearts we find ourselves walking to the river and taking off our shoes.

2. *CRITICISM*

One pastor expressed it this way, "Criticism is one of the things that really hurts. Amazingly, people will criticize their pastor in ways they would not speak of their worst enemy, and they feel they have a right to hold an opinion on everything the pastor does — his professional life, his emotional life, the way he dresses, his choice of words, his kids, his personality, the car he drives, the friends he chooses, and the list goes on. It's easy to feel like you're a constant disappointment to people, that you are letting people down all the time." We ask ourselves the question, "Is this the way I want to spend the rest of my life?"

I felt this deeply during my 20-year season of being a lead pastor. During this time, I constantly struggled with the feeling that I didn't have what people wanted and that I was always disappointing them. I've had people angry with me because of my poor memory, because of my choice of a word or an illustration in a sermon, because they saw me as too controlling or not controlling enough, because of the vacation I took, or because I couldn't be their friend. The list could go on and on.

Sometimes I found myself cringing when certain intercessors would come up to me, because I knew they were going to tell me some way in which I was disappointing God or disappointing the church. I knew their hearts were pure and right before God, but they had absolutely no comprehension of what I was walking through and dealing with; they didn't understand what the power of an encouraging word might have meant at that moment.

Besides the criticism we face in the church, our society as a whole has come to devalue the minister. When I first began in ministry, to be a minister had a general esteem attached to it. Ministers were seen as serving the community good. That is gone now. Ministers are often portrayed as hypocrites. If you watch a television show and there is a minister as one of the characters, you can almost guarantee that he is the villain or at least will be shown to have no integrity and to be hiding some awful secret. The brainwashing is so complete now, that when people are given surveys to rank professions, ministers are now just above car salesmen. The lack of respect can be painful when you are sacrificing so much for people.

It is easy to find myself walking to the river in my heart, taking off my shoes and placing them on the river shore. I just want to disappear. I never have actually quit, but in my heart, there is a part of me that sometimes longs for escape.

3. PERSONAL REJECTION AND BETRAYAL

One pastor expressed it this way, "It's painful to realize that people leave the church because they don't like you. That you can invest deeply in a person, but they can still come to the conclusion that they should leave the church because of something they don't like about you. And often they don't feel the need to even explain. They just stop coming."

I've always tried to be very open-handed with people who attended my church. Often when people joined the church, I would say something like, "We are thrilled that you are joining our church, but I want you to know that someday you will likely leave the church and that we are just as committed to making your leaving be as successful a transition for you as we have been in welcoming you."

Yet even though I tried to make it acceptable for people to leave, sometimes it seemed like people felt that they needed to show a good reason for why they were leaving. Sometimes it seemed like they felt constrained to show why the church was defective, to justify their decision to leave. They could have left in peace, simply saying that their family's needs had changed, but instead they felt a need to totally discredit the church. This can be very painful. I hate the feeling of going down an aisle at Walmart and seeing someone notice me who had burned bridges with the church like this and watching them jump to another aisle to avoid me.

Stories of betrayal abound — when family members hurt us, even family members who are part of the church; when ministry coworkers use their position to hurt you or hurt the church. I've had people use their gift of prophecy to declare what they thought were my faults. I've had people with a prophetic gift who told me that if I didn't conform to what they felt was supposed to happen in the church that God would eliminate me; He would just take me out.

King David understood this kind of betrayal. In Psalm 55: 12-14 he said, "For it is not an enemy who reproaches me, then I could bear it; nor is it one who hates me who has exalted himself against me, then I could hide myself from him. But it is you, a man my equal, my companion and my familiar friend; we who had sweet fellowship together walked in the house of God in the throng."

The sting of this kind of rejection comes and hits us, and there is a part of us that makes our way down to the river, takes off our shoes and carefully lays them down, wanting to disappear.

4. *LOW PAY*

A ll of us would like to earn more money, but that's not what I'm talking about. I'm talking about low pay that comes from giving yourself in a small community or to a ministry with few resources — low pay that can eat away at your self-esteem and that can create bitterness in your family; low pay that grinds away at us over a long period of time.

It could be caused by an immature church board that doesn't understand the power of blessing the pastor. Sometimes there is no money just because the money is not there — the ministry is just beginning or the community you're reaching is under-resourced. Possibly our lack is caused by our own stupid self-management and poor purchasing decisions that we've made. But however it's caused, the constant lack does something to us that brings us to that place of wanting to quit.

Depending on our background, we may see our pay as a measure of our personal worth. This ungodly belief tells us that higher paid people are more valuable people, and lower paid people have less value. I can remember that when I first told my family that I felt a call to ministry, several of them told me that I would never earn much money doing ministry. In their value system, I was choosing a path that reduced my potential in life.

Lack of money is a giant that can mock you and drive you to the river seeking escape.

5. BURNOUT

Ministry can be terribly draining, especially before we develop the skills to manage our time and the boundaries to say "no" when it is appropriate. I remember early in my ministry, I started an outreach to single adults called Mobilized To Serve. This conference ministry caught fire, and I suddenly found myself in great demand to speak all over the country. I was traveling every weekend. For a time, I traveled over 50% of the time. When I was home, I was in the office leading the conference planning team. My wife and I had young children, and the strain was starting to show.

One weekend I thought that I was scheduled to be home, but suddenly I realized I had made a mistake on my calendar and that I was actually scheduled to be away another weekend. I snapped. I started throwing things around my office and pounding my fists on my desk. It felt like the natural elastic that everyone has in their souls that lets them be flexible got stretched out to the point that it couldn't pull back into its proper place.

When you feel like that, it can feel like the river is the only place that you can go, that quitting is the only escape.

6. *DISAPPOINTMENT*

A minister's marriage can lose its way; the one place that you were hoping to find refuge becomes another battleground. Sometimes our children are hurt by our response to the ministry or by the immature response of people that we serve; as a result, we find them not following the Lord, and our hearts are filled with painful disappointment.

Sometimes our disappointment is the reality that we are not having the success in our ministry for which we had hoped. One time the youth pastor of our church was putting together a major outreach in our town park. The youth ministry team under his leadership was organizing a Battle of the Bands, with all kinds of local bands playing and most of them having a wholesome message of Christ's love. His dream was to have this tremendous outreach with a meaningful impact.

They had set up little tents, had gotten people to donate old furniture, and were putting couches all over the park. So much work had gone into this, from organizing the bands to the staging and moving all the furniture. On the morning before the evening of the event, after all the set up was done, it began to rain. It rained and it rained, and it rained all day.

We had the smell of moldy furniture around the church for weeks after that event, because they had to tear everything down soaking wet. The event, of course, did not have near the attendance and impact that the youth ministry team had hoped for. Who do you complain to? Is there somebody around here who controls the weather? God knew; couldn't He have protected us from this?

A disappointment like this can be overwhelming. The youth pastor and his team had given so much. When young people under your leadership face shattered expectations like this, it just rips your heart out. It is so easy to just find yourself saying, "What is the use? I think I'll just go down to the river and take off my shoes."

7. ENVY

It is difficult facing that other ministers seem to be progressing and you are being left behind. Their churches or ministries are prospering and yours is not. Their kids have made good choices and yours have not. You're facing envy in your heart, and you hate yourself because it's there.

Envy is the pain or distress caused by another person's success. You might think envy is not in the church, but the truth is envy is in people all through the Bible — Joseph's brothers, Sarah and Hagar, Rachel and Leah, Jesus' disciples, and the list goes on and on. The Bible even says that the reason the religious leaders crucified Jesus was because of envy. The truth is that when my personal worth is measured by my achievements, position, or possessions compared to others, I can become ensnared by envy.

It is easy to develop a view of life that says there is only a limited amount of good to go around. If another person prospers, it is always at my expense because whatever they have, I cannot have. As believers in Jesus Christ, we know that this kind of thinking is wrong — God has an endless supply — but it can still get a foothold in our lives. You can recognize it when you drive by a certain church, and when the shadow of that church falls across your car, you feel heat on that side of your face. You receive an email from a certain ministry, and you delete it with a certain extra enthusiasm — not because you don't need the information but because you are moved by envy toward the sender.

You hate that envy is in you, but it is there. And the battle with it drives you to the river, where you want to leave your shoes and slip away.

8. *PERSONAL BROKENNESS*

I think of a prominent Christian leader who was abused as a child, and he carried baggage his whole life that finally brought him down. He was brought down by his undealt-with brokenness. There are many others who have been brought up in dysfunctional homes. The truth is none of us grew up in perfect families, even those of us who came from Christian families, but some of us know the sting of alcoholism or drug abuse or maybe the ache of neglect in our family. And with that, we inherited certain brokenness, and even though Christ has saved us, redeemed us and done incredible things in our hearts, these experiences can still cause hurting, festering places in our lives that create control issues and trust issues in us.

I came from a broken family. My father left when I was 4 years old, and I had very limited contact with him as I was growing up. At the time I didn't see myself as broken at all, but now it is clear in my mind that I was. We have all been created to survive, so we try to come up with an approach to life that works for us. But what I discovered is that a solution may work for one season in life but not in another. The triggering event for me was when my first child was born. I could see that I had emotional attachment issues that needed to be processed. I knew that if I didn't address these issues, my relationship with my child would be distant. During this time of processing, I wanted to quit.

Maybe it is not what others have done to us but simply our own sin — our own foolish, stupid choices that we have made. One issue that many ministers are struggling with is pornography. We find ourselves filled with that hollow feeling after we involve ourselves in something that we know we should not be involved in.

We want the pain to stop. We don't want to keep going. We find ourselves wishing we could just leave our shoes at the river and disappear.

9. *A BARREN SOUL*

It's amazing to me that, though I serve God, I can grow so far from Him — that I can so easily lose my sense of personal relationship with the Lord. As a pastor, I stand up front in the church on Sunday morning for the purpose of stirring and encouraging others. I am commissioned to build up the body of Christ and to fulfill what I have felt called to do since I was 17 years old. It is amazing to me that sometimes I can find myself doing this great work with an absolutely barren soul. I find myself serving Christ as if He is not my friend, but that I'm a servant with no sense of personal relationship. When you encounter this level of spiritual dryness for a sustained period of time, it can be easy to think about quitting.

I can't help but think of the words of an old Keith Green song, "My Eyes Are Dry."

> *My eyes are dry; my faith is old*
> *My heart is hard; my prayers are cold*
> *And I know how I ought to be:*
> *Alive to You and dead to me*
> *But what can be done for an old heart like mine?*
> *Soften it up with oil and wine*
> *The oil is You, Your Spirit of love*
> *Please wash me anew with the wine of Your blood*

I think of the old oil pumps that I've driven by in the fields of northern Pennsylvania. You see this pump going up and down, up and down, pulling oil from the ground...at the same time as the pump is screaming because is in desperate need of being oiled itself. It is pumping away while it is screaming out, "Somebody please give me oil!"

We come to face this barrenness in our soul, and we wonder, "Is this what ministry is all about?" We want to sneak away. So, we make our way to the river, we take off our shoes, and we carefully place them in a way that says we are not here anymore.

The list of reasons that people in ministry quit is larger than what I've included here. We could also talk about loss of vision and a half a dozen other issues, but I believe that all of these obstacles will bow before Jesus Christ once we learn how to draw upon His empowerment.

We overcome the temptation to abandon our call to ministry when we FACE THESE ISSUES AND FIND GOD IN THEM.

Whether you find yourself like David, at 47 years of age staying home when the kings go out to battle and staring down from his rooftop at a beautiful woman. Or like Elijah, burned out after a great victory and filled with the fear of man that leaves you depressed and suicidal. Or like Moses, who allows himself to be so overcome with frustration with the people he is leading that he commits an outburst of anger, a work of the flesh that destroys his ability to lead. Or like Eli, who realizes he loves his sons more than he loves God and they are now hurting God's kingdom.

You may find, like these past leaders, that you need an encounter with God today, a transformation. The truth is that you have been down to the river — and though you have not yet gone beyond the thought in your heart, you're concerned that it could turn into an action of leaving your shoes by the water and walking away. Don't go another day without getting the encounter you need to break the power of this temptation to quit. Perseverance is challenging in any walk of life, but ministry leaders have a great warfare aligned against them.

3 Keys to Overcoming the Temptation to Quit

I want to share with you 3 key ideas, backed by Scripture, that have helped me to persevere when the pressure to quit has been strongest.

1. *REFRAME MY UNDERSTANDING OF MINISTRY*

Reframing is when you see an old thing in a new way that gives a positive light to it. Let me give a picture of how this works.

Sometimes I'm walking down the street in a downtown commercial section or in the mall, where the glass windows and doors are all along your side as you're walking. I look over out of the corner of my eye into the glass, and I see the reflection of this old man walking along. I think to myself, "Whoa, who's that old guy?" I'm thinking he'd look better if he lost a few pounds, and he would probably feel better about himself too. Then all at once I'm shocked as it hits me, "That guy is me!!" Sometimes I'll even stop, much to the embarrassment of my wife, as I realize I walk weird; I'm getting that old man shuffle. All of this is making me feel pretty bad about myself.

Well, one day I'm in the mall feeling bad about myself as I'm contemplating my reflection, and I see this guy walk in wearing a t-shirt that says on the front of it, "Aged to Perfection." He has a little strut when he walks, and I think to myself, "I like that! Yes, I am older, but I'm wiser than I used to be, I'm more experienced, and I'm seeing a lot of positives in my life. I've been down on myself for getting older, but maybe I'm wrong; maybe this is the good times, maybe this is harvest time. I'm 'Aged to Perfection!' I like it."

You see what is happening here is I'm reframing the idea of getting older. It has gone from becoming an old man to being "Aged to Perfection." This is not a delusion or me trying to tell myself a lie to encourage myself. Aging to perfection is a legitimate perspective on reality. I'm not just getting older; I'm getting better.

We must do this same kind of reframing when it comes to our thoughts about ministry, because the reality is that many of us have thoughts about ministry that are absolutely off the wall. Thoughts like... a minister should always be available... a minister is more spiritual than everybody else... a minister doesn't need friends... ministry to others is more valuable to God than ministry to my family... any problems a minister has is a lack of faith... a minister should not reveal their need. The list could go on and on.

And unless these thoughts get reframed, they will inevitably lead you to the river. It's like they box you in, so that your only path leads you to the river. It's going to happen if you keep thinking that way. This is why I've had to reframe my thoughts about ministry and why I want to share with you what I've learned.

The verse that helped me get a fresh perspective and triggered change for me is Acts 20:28. Paul is speaking to the Ephesian elders before he goes on to Rome and he says, "Be on guard for yourselves and for all the flock, among which the Holy Spirit has made you overseers, to shepherd the church of God which He purchased with His own blood."

"Be on guard for yourselves," he tells them. If you had asked me for a definition of ministry in my early days, I would have just said, "Loving God by caring for others." But now I've got a new t-shirt. Ministry has been reframed for me.

This is my new definition of ministry, and it has 3 elements to it:

1) Ministry is **loving God by caring for others.**

2) Ministry is **loving God by caring for my family.**

3) Ministry is **loving God by caring for myself.**

Ministry carries with it all three of these components, and if somehow they become separated, what you experience is not true biblical ministry, but a distortion. It is like a three-legged stool: if one leg is gone and you sit on the stool, you will fall over.

Take a moment and repeat these three sentences out loud:

Ministry is loving God by caring for others.

Ministry is loving God by caring for my family.

Ministry is loving God by caring for myself.

People who are in ministry are not just 8AM–5PM people; they are not just Monday–Friday people. Ministry demands our whole lives, which is why it is critical that we define ministry as containing all three of these elements, because the wrong definition of ministry could leave my family and my own self-care totally off the job description of Christian leader.

I don't think the first part of the definition, "Ministry is loving God by caring for others," needs explanation here, as it is probably where most of us start out. So let's talk about the often ignored other two legs of the stool.

Ministry is loving God
by *CARING FOR MY FAMILY*

"**M**inistry is loving God by caring for my family" is such a powerful concept. When a church or ministry hires you, they have also hired you to take care of your family — because if your family is not cared for, it destroys your ministry and minimizes your impact. What could have a greater negative impact on a church or organization than a leader's children growing up hating and resenting what the leader does? What can take the momentum out of a ministry faster than the leader's marriage dissolving?

As my kids were growing up, my wife and I made a commitment that we would do all that we could do to attend their sports games. Now I didn't go to every game; sometimes I was out of town. It wasn't like some unreasonable legalistic thing, but if there was any way that we could, we would go to their games. We just felt it was a priority for us to be there.

Every May, when the local Little League baseball season was happening, Elim Fellowship hosted a large ministers' conference, that I helped to organize. Hundreds of ministers would attend from around the country, and for the attendees this was a great "get-away from home and seek God" time. But for me, since I live in Lima where Elim is located, I also still had all the normal events of life happening, like mowing the lawn and fixing a broken car, and my kids had ballgames during the week of the conference. As a result, sometimes I would come a little late to the conference meetings. There were other times that I rescheduled church leadership meetings or rearranged ministry appointments, so I could attend one of my kids' games.

Someone could have said to me, "Going to your kids' games is not ministry. It is actually interfering with ministry." But they would have been dead wrong! Ministry is loving God by caring for my family, and one of the greatest gifts I could ever have given my church was children who knew they were loved and had a positive view of ministry and living in a pastor's home.

Understand me now — I'm not talking about the idolatry of family that Eli, for example, experienced where he put his family above God, and he wanted the approval of his children so much that he refused to discipline them. I'm not talking about the unwillingness to make sacrifices. My family has made many sacrifices. I've traveled around the world, and there were literally years of our family life when I was physically gone six months of the year in itinerant ministry. I remember during these times of travel, I was very concerned for my family. I was afraid that I would lose them. The Lord reassured me and said, "If you have to leave your family because of obedience to My call, you can be sure that I will care for your family. But if you offer your family up on the altar of your own ambition, then they can be hurt. Always be sure you are doing what I'm asking you to do, and everyone will be protected."

Yes, there were times I had to be away, but my wife and I made those decisions together. Occasionally, we did not have peace about a specific trip, and I would not accept it. At other times, I would have to be away a month at a time, but God met all of our needs and made it a joyful experience. I'm amazed today to hear my adult children talk about their childhood in a minister's house; there is no sense of resentment or suffering, but rather a sense that we were called together. When we are genuinely serving God, His grace is beyond amazing.

So maybe you've made mistakes in the past. That's okay. The past is past. We can't choose for yesterday or tomorrow, but we can choose for right now. You can make a choice today to reframe your definition of ministry, to write a new t-shirt.

Ministry is loving God
by *CARING FOR MYSELF*

A ministry that blesses others, strengthens my family, *and* pumps me up is the will of God for my life. That is my destiny. That is what God wants for me.

Godly assertiveness involves the confidence to know what is mine and to claim that without getting angry. Many people see any blessing that comes to them as selfish. The truth is when we claim what God has promised us, it glorifies Him. I'm telling you right now, what God has promised you as a minister of the Gospel includes the need to take care of yourself. You need to take care of your family and you need to take care of others, but you can't forget the third leg of the stool: to care for yourself.

Ministry has to be reframed in our mind away from this idea that ministry is only caring for others. Yes, ministry is others care. Ministry is also family care. And ministry is self-care. When I give time to all three values, I'm making a valuable investment, and I need to be assertive enough with whoever is interacting with me to explain the real definition of ministry. This is something God has given to me that I must do. I must claim what is my true call to ministry.

You can also see by this new definition of ministry, I have come to understand that when I give energy to my vacation, my hobbies, my education, my devotional life, and everything that nurtures my soul, I'm fulfilling my call to ministry. Many people see these things as somehow other; it's like I have the ministry and then my hobby is other. Or I have the ministry and my education is other. No, anything that nourishes my soul is helping fulfill my call to ministry.

I remember the year that I turned over the leadership of the church that I had pastored for 20 years to a young man on my staff. He was 27 years old. As I did it, I was believing that he would be the first fruits of many young ministers and leaders that I would have the opportunity to influence in the years to come. But the fact was, during the year that the transition was happening, I was going through all kinds of emotions — emotions that I didn't know how to define, express or even reflect on. It always amazes me when I meet an emotionally intelligent person who has a feeling and they can articulate what that feeling is. Sometimes I have a feeling and I don't even have words to talk about it.

My wife would say, "What are you feeling?"

And after a long pause, with a strained look on my face, I would say, "I don't really feel like I'm feeling anything."

"You're not being honest with me."

"Honey, it is much sadder than you think. You think I'm denying the truth, but I honestly don't feel anything."

I knew stuff was happening, but I didn't know how to express it. Your soul searches for ways to process things that don't fit into words. I couldn't tell you how what I'm about to tell you got started, but here is the story of what happened and how I processed leaving my job after 20 years as lead pastor.

I announced in January that I was leaving as the church's senior pastor at the end of that year, so that we could give everyone time to process the change. (One of the lessons I teach Christian leaders is a simple formula that has never failed me: communication + time = united change. If people know what is coming and they are given time to work through their feeling about it, more often than not they are able to make the change with you.) The process was working, but I didn't realize that one of the people who most had the need to process was me!

It was in August when I decided I was going to buy a scooter. My reasoning was that it would enable me to save gas. So, I start studying scooters and before I know it, I'm looking at motorcycles. But I'm super cheap, so I'm only thinking of a small motorbike that I can use around town. I'm searching Craigslist and reading articles about motorcycles and searching through all kinds of websites. I'm trying to figure out how

I can fulfill this desire that's building inside of me to have a motorcycle in the cheapest way possible. So, I decide that I'm going to buy an old motorcycle and fix it up, an old Honda Nighthawk 250. You motorcycle guys, don't laugh at me; I really liked my little 250.

Now my wife, understandably, was a little confused. I'm 54 years old and haven't driven a motorcycle or even expressed an interest in a motorcycle in our whole married life. My wife is looking at me and asking, "Are you okay?"

"I'm fine, Honey. I'm fine. Everything's fine."

"You've never wanted a motorcycle before, and now you want to set up our garage so you can work on it. Since when do you work on motorcycles? What are you thinking? What's happening? Explain to me."

I couldn't explain to her for the life of me what was going on. I didn't relate it to what was happening in the church or the redefining of who I was as I stepped away from my position in the church. All I knew was I had this burning passion to get an old motorcycle and start tearing it apart to fix it up.

And so, I start hanging out in our garage. I buy one motorcycle. I tear it apart. I fix it up. I drive it around. I sell it. I buy another one. The second one I buy had been kept in a garage, where mice had gotten into it and eaten all the wires. I had to go through every wire and find where it was connected and put a new wire in, stripping the ends, attaching it to the old wire, wrapping it with tape, and then move on to the next wire. I'm stripping down bike parts and polishing them and recoating them. I'm doing all of this in my garage. "Where's Dad?" "He's in the garage."

My wife is saying, "You want to spend more money on a motorcycle? You're buying what for the motorcycle?" And I'm saying, "Honey, let me go. Just let it go." I said this because I can't explain what is happening, but I know this must happen. I'm like a lemming going over a cliff.

I finish working on this motorcycle and I fix it up for myself to keep. Then I buy another one for $250 and rebuild the whole thing, cause I'm thinking one of my sons will ride it. Then I buy another one, so I can try and talk my wife into learning how to ride a motorcycle. As I'm going through this, I'm reading books. I'm looking at motorcycle mechanic websites. I'm scraping my knuckles. I'm not a mechanic. I've never done mechanical things my whole life. I've got the repair manuals to guide me.

During all this time, my garage is becoming my Fortress of Solitude. For those who don't know the Superman back story, the Fortress of Solitude is the place where he retreats between missions. It is the place where he goes when he is confused and needs to reconnect with the wisdom and mission with which he was sent to earth. Somehow my garage becomes a Fortress of Solitude for me, and as I'm scraping my knuckles and processing my emotions, the foundation is being laid in my soul so that we can have a successful transition from one lead pastor to another. What seemed like a horrible waste of time turned into the foundation for a successful transition for me, for my family, and for the church.

Sometimes we can feel it is wrong to assert our need and to do something to meet it. We think that a true minister of the Gospel should only think about other people's needs. The problem with this kind of thinking is that, unless I have the ability to assert my need, ultimately no one gets taken care of and a lot of people can end up getting hurt. Godly assertiveness involves the confidence to know what is mine in a healthy way, and to claim that without getting angry, demanding or defensive. Many people see any blessing that comes to them as selfish. The truth is when we claim what God has promised us it glorifies Him.

Ministry is loving God by caring for others.
Ministry is loving God by caring for my family.
Ministry is loving God by caring for myself.
You cannot separate these three concepts without destroying the minister.

2. *TRUSTING IN THE WISDOM OF GOD*

Daniel 2:20 says, "Let the name of God be blessed forever and ever, for wisdom and power belong to Him." God is wise. To make it long-term in the ministry so that all of our experiences at the river can be converted into internal transformation, you have got to come to the place of embracing and trusting in the wisdom of God.

Here is a definition of the wisdom of God that has helped me tremendously: "The wisdom of God tells us that God will bring about the best possible results, by the best possible means, for the most possible people, for the longest possible time." (Chip Ingram). That is the wisdom of God, and God uses His wisdom and power to accomplish His will.

This kind of thinking runs directly contrary to the experience of our lives. I've talked with a Christian man whose daughter was raped at college. Another friend shared about a grandchild with a birth defect. Still another told me how she was hanging on for God to restore her marriage, but her former spouse had just remarried. The truth is that God in His wisdom doesn't save us from trials. So, what is the highest good He is working for with His wisdom?

Well, the Bible tells us what the will of God is: the will of God is that you would be conformed to the image of His Son. Romans 8:28-29 says, "And we know that God causes all things to work together for good to those who love God, to those who are called according to His purpose. For those whom He foreknew, He also predestined to become conformed to the image of His Son, so that He would be the firstborn among many brethren."

God doesn't create problems to help people grow. He doesn't tempt people to sin. But God uses everything that touches our lives to cause us to become more like Christ. God uses His wisdom and power to help us become conformed to the image of His Son.

The will of God is not just the location where you are. The will of God is not just the people with whom you are working. The will of God is not even just the ministry to which you are called. The will of God is that whatever touches your life will touch you in such a way that you will become conformed to the image of His Son. And He uses His wisdom to massage our circumstances in such a way that He brings about the character of Christ in us. Remember: "The wisdom of God tells us that God will bring about the best possible results, by the best possible means, for the most possible people, for the longest possible time."

Now if you're like me, you probably have a lot of questions about your ministry. For example, those of you who are pastors might ask, "Why did God send me to this town?" Have you ever asked that question? I pastored for 20 years in Lima, a one-traffic-light small town in western New York. I've wondered, why did God send me to a one-light town? Was I incapable of handling something bigger? I found myself questioning the wisdom of God.

Maybe you have some other questions: "What was this church split all about?" "Why can't I seem to grow this church?" "Why does the money never seem to get to where we want it?" "Why does my board oppose me?" Friend, at some point you have to trust in the wisdom of God. The wisdom of God says that every struggle you've been going through has been helping to work into your life the character of Jesus Christ. He's been shaping you through your circumstances — the same way that He shaped his own Son Jesus. Remember the words from Hebrews 5:8, "Although He was a Son, He learned obedience from the things which He suffered." If God allowed suffering to touch His Son, isn't it clear that He will shape us and teach us in the same way?

Here is something God wants you to know: If there were a kinder, faster or gentler way for Him to change you, He would be using it. If you understood His love for you, it would so blow your mind. God is looking down on you right now and He is saying, "If there were any other way to do what needs to be done in you, I would do it. If there were a kinder, faster or gentler way to see the character of Christ formed in you, I promise you I would be using it. I need you to trust in My wisdom."

It is this embracing the wisdom of God that enables you to say, like Joseph as he reassured his brothers in Genesis 50:20, "As for you, you meant evil against me, but God meant it for good in order to bring about this present result, to preserve many people alive." Joseph was betrayed by family. He was falsely accused. He was forgotten in jail. But in the end, he could see that God had a plan all along.

Remember Paul and his thorn in the flesh? He asks the Lord three times to remove it, but the Lord answers him in 2 Corinthians 12:9, "My grace is sufficient for you, for power is perfected in weakness." Paul had to surrender to the wisdom of God.

When I understand the wisdom of God, my circumstances don't necessarily change, but my view of God becomes clearer and my faith increases. This perspective is what drains away the bitterness, and bitterness has got to be drained out of us for us to survive in ministry. This is what enables us to not come to the end of ourselves and quit. We come to the realization that God, in His wisdom, has been working all things together for our good. He's been shaping the character of Christ in us.

Jesus said it another way, while embracing the wisdom of God as He was nailed to that cross. He looked down at the people yelling horrible things at Him and He says in Luke 23:34, "Father, forgive them, for they do not know what they are doing."

Is there anyone who has hurt you in the ministry? Has that pain brought you to the river's edge with your shoes in your hand? The Lord is asking you right now, "Can you trust in My wisdom?" God didn't create the hurt you have faced. The simple reality is we live in a sin-sick world filled with brokenness and pain. But God has a promise for you, "If you trust in My wisdom, I will not allow one of your tears to be wasted. I will use these trials to shape in you the character of Christ, and what others have meant for evil, I will use for good in your life."

I often must remind myself of the wisdom of God when I'm in the midst of a trial. I have phrases that I replay in my mind to remind me to trust in Him. Here are some of the phrases; feel free to use them when you need to remind yourself that God is in control.

- God knows what He is doing.
- God is not trying to hurt me but to bless me.
- God will make me better through this.
- I want to be comfortable, but God wants me to grow.
- This is not a mistake. God will use this to change me.
- God will not waste my pain.
- What others have meant for evil, God has meant for good.
- If I sow in tears, I will reap in joy.
- God never promised me a trouble-free life; He promised to make me like Jesus.

God wants you to know that your Heavenly Father constantly searches to redeem the circumstances that touch your life, so that they work for your good — now and in eternity.

3. *BE POURED OUT AS A DRINK OFFERING*

Here is how Paul describes it in Philippians 2:17. "But even if I am being poured out as a drink offering upon the sacrifice and service of your faith, I rejoice and share my joy with you all." In 2 Timothy, which is the last book that Paul wrote and likely reflects his last words to us, he says the same phrase again in chapter 4. "I'm being poured out as a drink offering." It's like a summing-up phrase for him.

Now when you see this expression "drink offering," you may wonder what it's talking about. I think one of the best biblical pictures of this is the story in 2 Samuel 23 of David in battle. As he looks at Bethlehem, which was being held by his enemies, he almost involuntarily verbalizes the cry of his heart — the longing to have a drink from the well of Bethlehem. His mighty men hear his deep desire and decide to do something about it. Three men rush into the enemy-held city, they leap over the wall, they go to the well and scoop out water from the well, and then they rush back through the city to escape. They risk their lives going into the center of enemy territory. They bring back the water and give it to David, which says more about their love and commitment to him in that one act than could have been said in a book of promises.

David takes the water and he says in essence, "I can't drink this. This water represents your lives. I am not deserving of your lives. This kind of sacrifice can only be given to God." Then he pours out their life-committed water before God, who alone was worthy of it. He gives it as a drink offering to God.

The Lord is worthy of your life being poured out for Him. You may look at the ministry God has given you and wonder, "Is it worth it?" "Is this small town worth the sacrifice that it demands of me to reach out to it?" Remember, it is not the place you are serving — it is the Lord you are serving. The Lord is worthy of your life being poured out.

Others may not understand; they may think that the price you are being asked to pay is too great. They may think that the impact you are making is not worth the effort and cost required to give. The truth is He is worthy of your life being poured out. No man could receive the sacrifice of your life in that way, but God is worthy of your very best.

The altar that you are being poured out on as you serve in ministry today is made up of three stones. Let's talk about these 3 stones.

1. The first stone of your altar is
THE LIMITATIONS OF YOUR GIFTS

There is no secret here; all of us have limitations to our gifting. It is only as the body of Christ works together that Jesus can be fully experienced by others. As individuals, each of us only has limited gifts, but as we work in unity with others the full picture of what Christ offers can be revealed to those who need Him. This is why — if we believe the lie that somehow we as the ministry leader are supposed to have all of the answers and be the most spiritual person on our team — we are setting ourselves up for frustration and disappointment. Failure is assured.

When you become aware of your limitations and weaknesses, you can't help but ask the question, "Why did God choose me as a leader?" Maybe you're not the best speaker; maybe you're not the best administrator. But you are the leader that God chose for your community and your organization; He did it. This is humbling to acknowledge but life-saving at the same time. It is humbling, because we secretly think that our leadership is somehow rooted in our superpower. The truth is that even our best strengths and giftings are not enough for us to do the job of leadership to which God has called us.

It is only when we allow ourselves to humbly give our best — acknowledging that it is not enough — that God steps in and uses the gifts of the whole team, plus supernatural favor, to demonstrate that it is He who is really doing the work. This is the life-saving part, because if we don't understand that our strengths are not enough, our tendency is to double down on our strength, thinking that we only need to do more. So we sacrifice our family and we sacrifice ourselves, thinking that just a little more effort will win the day. As a result, our family, our ministry, and ourselves get destroyed.

You can look at it all day long and think, "I wish I were this; I wish I were that; I wish I were someone other than who I am." But the fact is that He knew what your town needed,

He knew what your ministry required, and He says, "Trust in My wisdom and I will accomplish My purposes—if you will allow yourself to be poured out on this altar, the altar of your limited gifts."

2. The second altar stone God is asking you to be willing to be poured out on is *THE LIMITATIONS OF YOUR MISSION*

If you are a pastor, it may be the community you're trying to reach. If you're a ministry head, it may be the specific challenges you face trying to fulfill your mission. God puts some people in cities; He puts some in very restricted neighborhoods. Some are focused on hard people groups, and some are facing huge financial challenges. He puts some of us in communities where everybody is ready to say yes to God and some of us in places where no one is ready to say yes.

We must yield to the fact that God is in charge and He chooses the mission to which you are assigned. We must surrender to His Lordship and give Him permission to send us where He wants us to go, to do what He wants us to do. Our mission says nothing about us and everything about the God we serve. Our mission is not a reflection of our worthiness or the strength of our gifting. Sometimes God uses the foolish things to confound the wise. Sometimes He wants to show His extravagant love in a situation by using a person of incredible gifting to do what humanly appears to be an insignificant task. In both situations, the servant serves at the pleasure of the Master, and the mission says nothing about the worth of the servant. We cannot choose our mission; we can only choose our Master. We do not choose success or failure; we can only choose obedience or disobedience.

God has formed an altar for you, and He is saying to you, "Am I worthy for you to be poured out as a drink offering before me on this altar stone of your mission?"

3. The third altar stone God is asking you to be poured out on is the altar of *THE LIMITATIONS OF YOUR TEAM*

Why did God give you the worship leader you have, or the elder, or the youth guy? Why do you have the board chairman you have or the executive team you have? Why not somebody better? Why not somebody with different abilities? Why not somebody who can see things more clearly? These are the people whom God gave you, even though they may not fulfill all of your aspirations. In His wisdom, He knew that they are exactly what you need — and you are what they need.

You can see the limitations of your team as something that is holding you back — or as something that is guiding you. Let's say I feel the need for a strong musician on the team and I work very hard to get a person with those gifts, but it just never works out. I can view that as keeping me from fulfilling my God-given mission. Or I can stop and ask myself these questions, "Why didn't God supply? Is it possible, if I don't have a strong musician, that God has another way for me to move forward with the team he has given me?"

There is an old adage that has guided me in many situations: "Where God guides, God supplies." When God is not supplying me with the human resources I think I need, I often stop and reassess my presuppositions about the ministry I'm leading. Are there methods that I have called God's will that really were just the way I thought He wanted things done, but He has a whole different way of accomplishing the mission?

The team He gives us doesn't limit us; it guides us. Is there someone on the team who seems extremely cautious, almost fearful? I can reject that limitation — or I can see it as a gift from God that can help me evaluate our next steps. Do I have a key volunteer whose time is limited? I can see that as holding us back — or is it possible that there is a timing involved in this mission that needs to be slowed down?

I'm not saying that we should have a "Whatever will be, will be" attitude. Work hard to get the best team you can, but often your team — even after your best efforts — will have limitations. I'm challenging you to see these limitations not as obstacles, but as God's special gift to you. Commit yourself to work with what God has given you, and in this way you become a drink offering poured out before the Lord.

The stone of your limited gifting, the stone of your limited mission, and the stone of your limited team: these form the altar that God is asking you to pour yourself out on.

God is asking you today, *"Am I worthy of your life being poured out as a drink offering to Me on the altar of these three stones?"*

WILL YOU SURRENDER TO GOD'S PLAN?

If you have been battling with quitting the ministry, would you do something for me right now? In your mind's eye, would you walk back to the water's edge? You have made the trip a few times before — not enough times yet to get up and quit what you are doing — but you have gone there enough times that you have a deposit there that anchors your soul to that temptation to quit.

I don't know what drove you there; only you know that. I don't know what has worked in your life or the pressures you've faced, the battles you have struggled with, the disappointments in leadership, or anything else that has touched you, but somehow you are connected to that place of quitting.

You have made your way to the river; you have dropped your shoes there, and there is a part of you that has walked away.

Will you trust in His wisdom? Are you able to embrace where He has you right now?

The Spirit of God is asking you today, "Will you put your shoes back on?"

Will you come before God today and say, "Father, I trust in Your wisdom and I'm willing to be poured out — even though I don't understand everything that is going on. If there were a kinder, faster, gentler way to make me like Jesus, I know You would use it. I trust in Your wisdom, and I'm willing to be poured out as a drink offering on the altar that You have made for my life. I'm not going to judge the altar because I'm trusting in Your wisdom. If, in Your extravagance, You have decided that I need to be poured out on these altar stones of limitation, I offer myself to You again willingly as I did once many years ago.

"I will put my shoes back on, and I say 'yes' to You. Pour me out. I'm not going anywhere. I'm not quitting. I'm not leaving. I'm going to let You finish the work that You've begun in me."

Did you reclaim your shoes from the river?

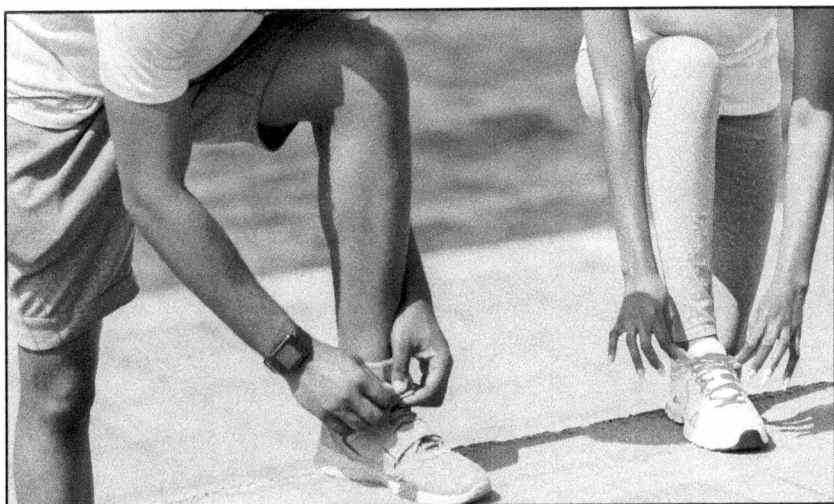

Resources

What is NOT MANY FATHERS about?

Many emerging Christian leaders have come into spiritual leadership with little experience or practical ministry training. In many cases, their home life had little spiritual grounding, and their formal training was secular. Yet they have had a powerful encounter with God and feel called to serve Him. Their call is real, but success is not guaranteed.

Now they need relationship with someone who has more ministry experience — a spiritual father to share experience, critical skills and inspiration for the mission they are facing. A mentor with a history of ministry experience and the heart of a spiritual father giving support during a leader's formative stages can greatly increase the possibility of a long-lasting and effective ministry.

> *For though you have countless guides in Christ,*
> *you do not have many fathers.* 1 Corinthians 4:15

Paul says in 1 Corinthians 4:15: "For though you have countless guides in Christ, you do not have many fathers." The mission of Not Many Fathers is to impart to others what God has given me and other spiritual fathers, encouraging them to accomplish more than we ever have — to help emerging Christian leaders in how to make wise life and leadership decisions, to preach dynamically, and to boldly launch their ministry visions so they can reach their God-given potential.

The tools we use to accomplish this are writing inspirational leadership development books that can be consumed in about an hour, and speaking in churches and conferences, along with classes, discipleship, and personal consulting that are done in person and online.

More resources from Mike Cavanaugh

Are you interested in reading more of Mike Cavanaugh's ministry-related books? Other titles include: *How to Lead Your Ministry through Change, How to Preach Effectively* and *Redefining Success for the Small Church.* All of these are available in ebook format at notmanyfathers.com or as printed books on Amazon.

No one starts out knowing everything they need to succeed. If you're not satisfied with what is happening in your ministry, these resources might be exactly what you need to strengthen the impact of God's calling in your life. Check out **notmanyfathers.com**. You can contact Mike at mike@notmanyfathers.com.

How to support this ministry

When people hear what Not Many Fathers is attempting to do, they often want to contribute to support the vision. Mike does not draw a salary, and all the expenses of the ministry are covered by Mike's traveling to speak, tuition from some classes he teaches, and the personal donations of people who want to invest in the vision or to say thank you for the free resources they have received.

If you're interested in giving financially, you can go to the website notmanyfathers.com and donate (donations are not tax-deductible). If you would like to give a larger gift and need a tax deductible receipt, please contact Mike at mike@notmanyfathers.com; he has tax exempt organizations associated with him that can provide a receipt for you.

If your church would like to support Not Many Fathers as part of its missions giving, Mike would be happy to meet with your board to explain the mission and thank them personally. The expenses of maintaining the website and publishing are real, and your help would be greatly appreciated.

Dedication

Throughout my adult life, there has been one person who has stood beside me in everything I have attempted and has given her all to support me in every behind-the-scene way possible. She is my wife, Terri. There is no ministry that I have given myself to that my wife has not made possible by working with me. Sometimes her work has been acknowledged with pay, and other times she has just done what needed to be done with no thought of herself. No ministry I've led would have succeeded without her personal sacrifice. I have often received the applause that she has deserved. At this season of my life, I feel nothing but overwhelming gratitude and love every time I look at her. What a fantastic partner she has been. In this series of books to help beginning ministers, she is my editor, layout and design person. I dedicate this whole series to her, and I thank God for every day that we can continue to partner together in life and ministry.

Mike Cavanaugh is the founder and director of Not Many Fathers, a ministry dedicated to mentoring emerging Christian leaders in how to make wise decisions, preach dynamically, and boldly initiate their visions so they can reach their God-given potential.

Mike was the founder and director of BASIC College Ministry, which after 40 years is still helping churches impact students for Christ. He also founded and directed Mobilized to Serve, which challenged single adults to serve Christ. During this time, he also wrote the book *God's Call to the Single Adult,* which has sold over 100,000 copies and is still published today under the title *The Power and Purpose of Singleness.*

Mike pastored Elim Gospel Church, a dynamic congregation of nearly 1,000 in Lima, NY, for 20 years, including leading them to raise the funds and construct a 60,000 sq.ft. ministry center. He has also served as the vice president of Elim Fellowship, a ministerial organization where he worked with hundreds of pastors, missionaries and Christian leaders.

Most recently, Mike served for 8 years as the president of Elim Bible Institute and College, where he led the school to achieve full accreditation and saw hundreds of thousands of dollars of aid released for students at the only accredited charismatic Bible college in New York.

He is a graduate of Elim Bible Institute and College, Roberts Wesleyan College, and Bakke Graduate University. Mike and his wife, Terri, reside in Lima, NY, and have three adult children and nine grandchildren.